The Early Years Foundatio

CW00531488

The Early Years Foundation Stage prepares children for learning at Key Stage 1 and is con_____ Curriculum. It focuses on the needs of children from birth to the end of the Reception year. The philosophy underpinning the Early Years Foundation Stage curriculum is that learning should be carefully planned and structured, with the emphasis on activities that are fun, relevant and motivating. The Everything Early Years books are written with this philosophy in mind.

The Practice Guidance for the Early Years Foundation Stage, published in 2007, is the core reference document for implementation of the Early Years Foundation Stage. Its aim is to give guidance for practitioners to meet the wide range of needs of all children.

For further information on the Early Years Foundation Stage:
www.teachernet.gov.uk/publications
or for a copy of the Guidance phone DCSF publications **0845 60 222 60**

The Outdoor Series Collection

This Outdoors series is suitable for older or more able Early Years Foundation Stage children and also in Key stage 1.

Authors:

Jo Visser (B.Ed. Hons) has been an early years teacher for over 10 years. She has been working in a curriculum advisory role.

Hilary Pauley (B.Ed.) is the Headteacher of Milton Keynes Preparatory School.
The activities in this Outdoors Series have been tried and tested in schools.

Illustrated by **Margaret Ramsbotham.**
Edited by **Lisa Pauley-Cordes.**
Cover photograph by **Lisa Pauley-Cordes.**
Resources lists by **Lisa Flynn.**
Recommended books by **Victoria Park Books www.victoriaparkbooks.co.uk**

Published by **Everything Early Years 2009.**

ISBN 978-1-904975-51-9

9 781904 975519 >

Everything Early Years
MKPS, Tattenhoe Lane, Milton Keynes, Bucks, MK3 7EG.
www.everythingearlyyears.co.uk
ISBN 978-1-904975-51-9

The Outdoor Series

Exploration and Investigation

Introduction

The key to this series is to remember that anything that can be done indoors can be taken outdoors, and there are so many more activities that only the space of the outdoors makes possible.

The Early Years Foundation Stage states *'being outdoors has a positive impact on children's sense of well-being and helps all aspects of children's development'*. The freedom and challenges of exploring and investigating outside in both adult led and child initiated activities offer holistic development opportunities.

You do not need to wait for good weather – take the opportunity all year round to use and explore the outdoors. Simple indoor tasks, such as the colouring table, can be taken outdoors, as well as the more complex activities, such as designing a water system using drainpipes. When it's raining splash in the puddles and listen to the rain drops. When it's sunny, build a sun shelter and make shadow puppets. When it's windy, fly home-made kites and move like a tree blowing in the wind. Only the outside area offers such an organic, dynamic environment which changes with the season and the weather to give a rich, wide and varied learning experience.

Make sure that the children have the opportunity to access and enjoy the outdoors every day. Guidance from the Early Years Foundation Stage states *'whenever possible, there should be access to an outdoor play area, and this is the expected norm for providers. In provisions where outdoor play space cannot be provided, outings should be planned and taken on a daily basis'*.

The use of outdoor space offers experiences to support many of the Early Learning Goals. For example:

- **PSED** – Continue to be interested, excited and motivated to learn.
- **PSED** – Be confident to try new activities.
- **CLL** – Interact with others, negotiating plans and taking turns.
- **CLL** – Enjoy listening to and using spoken language and readily turn to it in their play and learning.
- **PSRN** - Use language such as 'greater', 'smaller', 'heavier' or 'lighter' to compare quantities.
- **PSRN** - Talk about, recognise and recreate simple patterns.
- **KUW** – Investigate objects and materials by using all of their senses.
- **KUW** – Look closely at similarities, differences, patterns and change.
- **PD** – Show awareness of space, of themselves and of others.
- **PD** – Use a range of small and large equipment.
- **CD** - Respond in a variety of ways to what they see, hear, smell, touch and feel.
- **CD** - Express and communicate their ideas, thoughts and feelings by using a widening range of materials, suitable tools, imaginative and role-play, movement, designing and making, and a variety of songs and musical instruments.

The Outdoor Series: Exploration and Investigation, is a collection of 12 books:

- Construction
- Dens
- Wildlife
- Dance and movement
- Touch
- Messy play
- Water
- Music
- Jobs
- Hands on!
- Listening
- Small world play

Each book offers a range of activities on how to make the most of your outside space, whatever the weather. As well as the activities you will find:

- a clear outline of resources needed
- the specific early learning goals met in each activity
- key vocabulary to support their learning
- enrichment activities designed to stretch the older or more able children
- suggestions for more to explore and home links
- an observation sheet for your evaluations and comments.

This Outdoor Series title is suitable for older or more able EYFS children and those in KS1.

Contents

Introduction to Water

Children love playing and exploring in water, whether it is rain, ice or in the paddling pool. Water play encourages the children to enjoy the company of their peers, sharing equipment and taking turns in conversation. It encourages the children to be explorative, asking suitable questions and seeking the answers.

This book highlights water activities that specifically meet these Early Learning Goals:

- KUW ask questions about why things happen and how things work
- PD handle tools, objects and construction safely and with increasing control
- KUW look closely at similarities, differences, patterns and change
- PSED continue to be interested, excited and motivated to learn.

Water play should be available to the children everyday. It does not need to be a defined activity, it can be a free play opportunity.

Suitable resources for the water tray could include:

- Jugs of different sizes
- Funnels
- Cups
- Water wheels
- Sieves
- Food colouring
- Floating and sinking objects
- Tubing
- Buckets and brushes

Try varying the activities for the children. Try:

- Washing the dolls' clothes
- Washing the tea set
- Whisking bubbles
- Melting ice cubes in warm water
- Car Washing
- Doing the laundry
- Bathing the dollies

Investigating ice

What the children will learn:

- The children will have the opportunity to investigate ice using their sense of touch and sight

- They will realise that water changes once frozen then changes again as it melts

- They will enjoy working collaboratively

Early Learning Goals:

PSED – be confident to try new activities, initiate ideas and speak in a familiar group

KUW – investigate objects and materials by using all of their senses as appropriate

Useful Vocabulary:

- Water
- Freeze
- Ice
- Melt
- Cold
- Hot
- Wet

Key activity – ice, ice and more ice!

What you need:

- Water

- Different sized moulds to make ice cubes

- Large trays

What to do:

- In advance, ask the children to help you make different shaped ice cubes using the moulds

- Now, introduce the activity by reading 'Cuddly Dudley' by Jez Alborough and 'One Snowy Night' by Nick Butterworth

- Now, take the frozen ice outside on the trays.

- With a small group of children, talk about how the water has changed – i.e it is now cold and hard. Encourage them to use a descriptive vocabulary: freeze, cold, hard, etc

- Now, explore the ice. Ask questions such as how does it feel? What does it look like? What happens as it begins to melt?

- Try breaking some ice. What happens to the smaller pieces?

- Who can make their piece of ice melt the fastest?

- Describe the ice as it melts – does it stay hard? Why does it turn into water? Does it feel as cold as it did as ice?

- Try adding food colouring to water and making more ice cubes. What happens?

Investigating ice

More to explore

What you need:

- Fruit juice

- Ice lolly moulds

- Lolly sticks

What to do:

- Introduce the activity by reminding the children about the previous activity

- Now, talk about how ice cream and ice lollies cool us down on hot days!

- Explain that we are going to make our own ice lollies using the fruit juice

- Talk about the property of the fruit juice as a liquid – e.g you can pour it, it is runny, etc

- Ask the children to help you pour the fruit juice into the moulds and add the sticks

- Once frozen, talk about the changes in the fruit juice – for example, it is frozen, it is hard. Talk about other cold things. Snow is cold. Is it hard? What is snow? Does it melt?

- Now, enjoy the lolly!

Home links

- Make some ice cubes together at home. Share these when having a drink

- Go shopping to buy an ice lolly!

- At the supermarket, look at the food in the frozen section. Feel the temperature drop

- See what happens to ice when the tray is placed above a warm radiator

Investigating ice

Enrichment Activities

The properties of ice and water

What you need:

- Balloons

- Water and the water tray

- Sponge

- Sieve

What to do:

- Fill some balloons with water and freeze them

- Now take the water tray outside and fill with water.

- In small groups, investigate the water:
    - How do you know this is water?
    - What happens when you squeeze the sponge?
    - How does the water move through the sieve?

- Now, take the balloon outside, cut it and explore the ice:
    - How was this ice made?
    - Look closely at the pattern in the ice.
    - Would the ice be soaked up by the sponge?
    - What is the same about water and ice?
    - What is different?

- Wait for the ice to start to melt:
    - What is happening to the ice?
    - Why?
    - How can we make the ice melt faster? For example, leave in the sun.

- Conclude the experiment by writing a report about their investigation:
    - What can water do that ice cannot?
    - Describe the differences and similarities between water and ice.
    - How can we turn water into ice?
    - How doe ice turn back into water?

Weighing ice

What you need:

- Ice cubes

- Plastic bags

- Weighing scales

What to do:

- Place a large ice cube inside a plastic bag. Weigh it.

- Let the ice melt.

- Predict whether the water will weigh the same or more or less than the ice.

- Now weigh the water.

- Was their prediction correct?

Observations

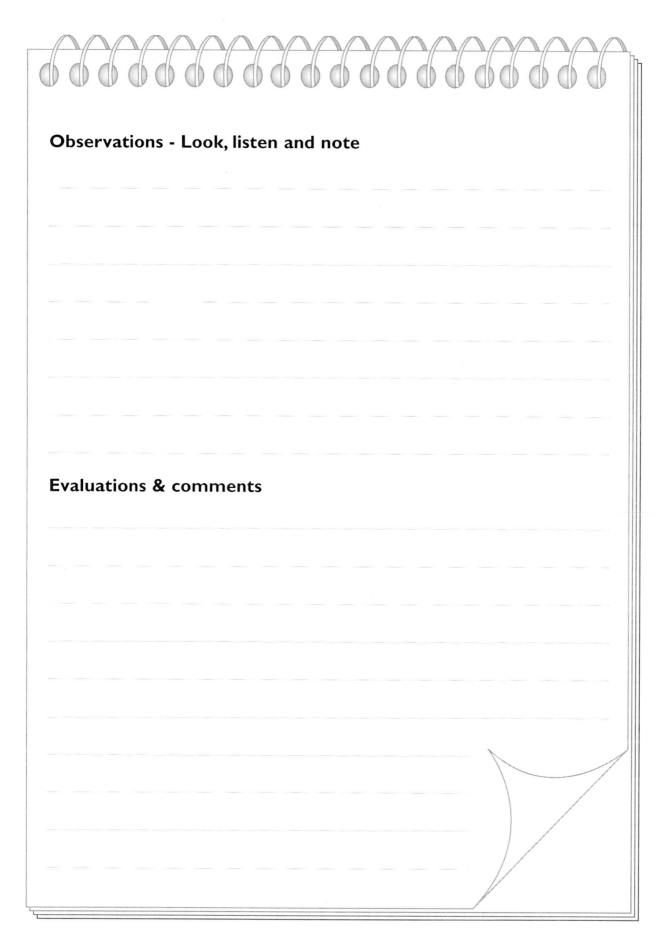

Observations - Look, listen and note

Evaluations & comments

Playing in the rain

What the children will learn:

- The children will enjoy the company of their peers

- They will use their large and fine motor skills

- They will learn about the changing weather

Early Learning Goals:

CLL – speak clearly and audibly, with increasing confidence

KUW – look closely at similarities, differences, patterns and change

PD – move with increasing control

Useful Vocabulary:

- Rain
- Puddle
- Splash
- Shower
- Wet
- Dry

Key activity – I'm singing in the rain!

What you need:

- A rainy day (or create your own puddles)

- Umbrellas

- Wellington boots

- Watering cans with a rose

What to do:

- Take the children outside, all dressed for the rain, with Wellington boots.

- Enjoy singing 'it's raining, it's pouring, 'Dr Foster went to Gloucester' and 'rain, rain go away'

- Now, encourage the children to explore the puddles – jump in them, splash, jump from one puddle to another, follow one another, etc

- Ask them to listen carefully to the sound of the rain – describe the sound we hear – pitter, patter, plop, splash. Keep a record of the words they use

- Try following one another's wet footprints – stand on their prints, make a circle with their wet prints, etc

- Develop this – on a dry day use the watering can and rose to create rain falling and making puddles

- Remind the children about the words they used to describe the falling rain

- Make a class display – using large raindrops with descriptive words written inside

Playing in the rain

More to explore

What you need:

- A recording of rain

What to do:

- Take the children outside with the recording of the rain
- Ask them to sit quietly and listen to the rain – encourage them to describe what they hear
- Now, show the children how to use their hands to clap – to represent a shower of rain
- Now, change the speed of the clapping to create a big thunder storm!
- Create a sequence – for example, a small shower started this morning, then by lunchtime it had turned into a huge storm, then slowly, but slowly, the storm subsided and turned back into a gentle shower
- Add some instruments to your storm: drums, a thunder tube, bells, triangles. Record your storm and play it to another class.

Home links

- Use the watering can to water the garden plants together
- Play with the kitchen sieves and colanders to make the sound of the rain
- Enjoy a shower!

everything
early years

Playing in the rain

Enrichment Activities

The rain gauge

What you need:

- Funnel

- Clear measuring jugs

What to do:

- Introduce the activity by talking about rainfall.

- Use diagrams to illustrate the weather cycle – talk about the moving air, the heat from the sun turning the water vapour from the sea. Then the cold air turning the vapour into clouds

- Now, ask the children to think about how we can find out how much rain has fallen

- Explain that they are going to keep a record of the rainfall over a period of time.

- In pairs, place a funnel into a clear measuring jug. Every time it rains, mark the water level onto the outside of the jug.

- After a period of time, look at the measurements. How much rain has fallen?

- Now plot these measurements onto a simple chart.

- Interpret the chart.

- How much rainfall did they observe over the period?

- Can they work out when it rained the most?

Materials and the rain gauge

What you need:

- Drainpipes

- Plastic jugs

- Cardboard tubes

What to do:

- Talk about the different ways we can collect rain.

- Ask the children to work together and design their own rain gauges. Provide them with different resources – drainpipes, plastic jugs, rulers,

- Add other materials such as cardboard tubes. Ask the children to think about why these are unsuitable resources.

- Test out their ideas. Would they like to make any changes? Is their gauge easy to read?

Observations

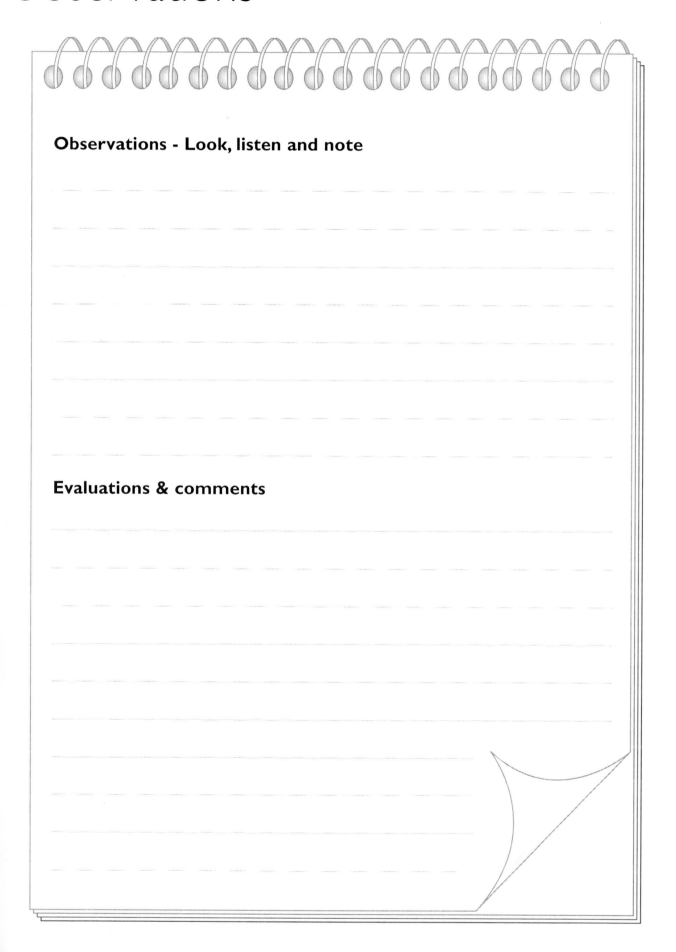

Observations - Look, listen and note

Evaluations & comments

everything
early years

Water painting

What the children will learn:

- The children will use their creative and imaginative skills

- They will enjoy the company of their peers, while developing their fine motor skills

Early Learning Goals:

PSED – form good relationships with adults and peers

KUW – ask questions about why things happen and how things work

PD – handle tools safely and with increasing control

Useful Vocabulary:

- Paint
- Water
- Dry
- Wet
- Pattern
- Soak
- Spray

Key activity – painting with water

What you need:

- Large paint brushes
- Sponges
- Spray bottles
- Buckets of water

What to do:

- Take the children outside with the large brushes, the sponges, rollers and the spray bottles
- Using the equipment, ask the children to use the water to 'paint' the schools walls, fences and the ground
- Make patterns and pictures – try making large circles, zigzags, straight and wavy lines, etc
- Try painting their initial letters from their names on the ground using the latter sounds. Can they recognise one another's initials?
- Try painting a track on the ground – follow one another's routes. Where do they end up?
- Now, explore what happens as the walls dry
- Develop this – take the painting easels outside. Encourage the children to enjoy free painting
- Enjoy printing with paints, sponges and rollers

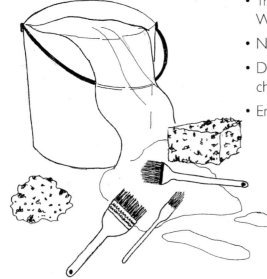

Water painting

More to explore

What you need:

- Water
- Water paints
- Easels
- Brushes

What to do:

- Take the children outside with the equipment
- Explain that you would like them to paint a picture of their choice using the water colours
- Show the children how to use the water and the paints effectively
- Talk about what they are painting and the colours they will need
- As they paint, watch the colours run and mix together. Do any of the colours change when they mix together?
- Leave the pictures to dry before displaying
- Paint a picture with the paper flat on the ground.
- Paint the same picture while the paper is on an easel. What is the difference? Can you see the water colour running down the paper? Which do you prefer?

Home links

- Use the sponge to wash at bath time. Look how the sponge absorbs the water. Squeeze the water back out the sponge
- Use different brushes at home – for example, the toothbrush, the broom and the hairbrush. How many can they find?
- Enjoy free painting together at home and in the garden.

Water painting

Enrichment Activities

Exploring evaporation

What you need:

- Water

- Chalk

- A sunny day!

What to do:

- Introduce the children to the concept of evaporation – a liquid changing into a gas.
- Now, outside, ask the children to pour some water on the ground to make some puddles.
- Ask the children to draw around their puddles with the chalk.
- Now, leave the puddles alone.
- Periodically, visit the puddle. If it has changed in size draw around the new shape.
- Remind the children to keep checking their puddles throughout the whole day.
- At the end of the day, discuss what has happened to the size of the puddle – explain that a puddle dries up because, due to the heat of the sun, the water evaporates and turns into water vapour.
- Ask them to predict what will happen to the puddle by the morning.
- Now, write up their experiment, using key headings:
  - What I needed.
  - What I did.
  - What happened?
  - Why this happened?
  - Draw a diagram to illustrate their experiment.
- Share their write-ups with one another

Observations

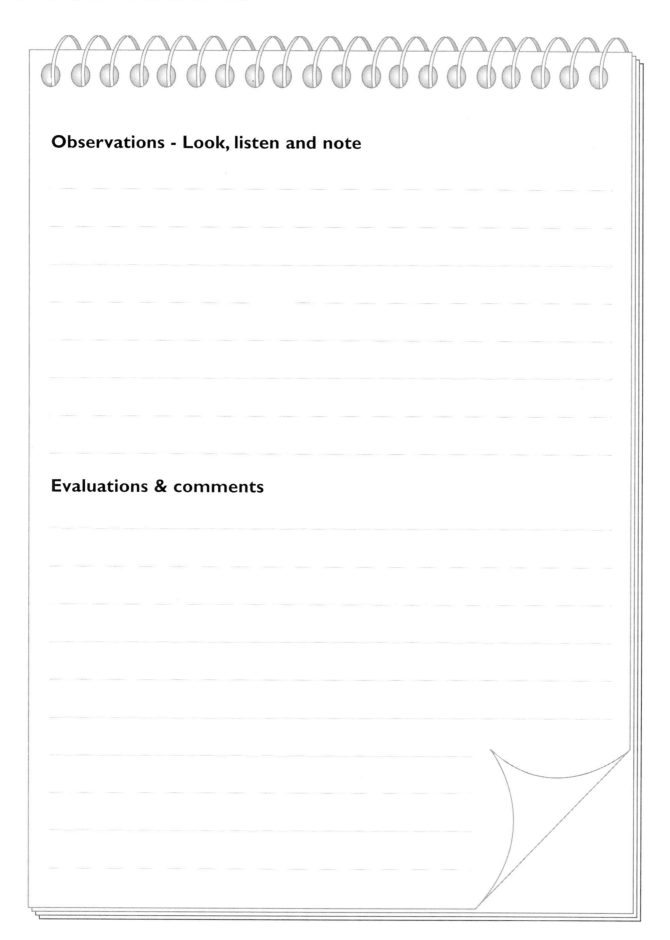

Observations - Look, listen and note

Evaluations & comments

Make a pond

What the children will learn:

- The children will be encouraged to work creatively

- They will share thoughts and ideas

- They will use a growing vocabulary

Early Learning Goals:

KUW – look closely at similarities, differences, patterns and change

PD – handle tools and construction safely and with increasing control

Useful Vocabulary:

- Pond
- Water
- Under
- On top
- Pond life
- Fishing
- Frogs, fish, ducks

Key activity – making a pond

What you need:

- A water tray

- Water

- Green food colouring
- Plastic ducks, fish and frogs

- Fishing nets

- Small pebbles and stones

What to do:

- Introduce the activity by singing '5 little speckled frogs'
- Look at pictures and reference books of different ponds, and if possible, visit one
- Now, put the water tray and resources into the garden
- With a small group of children, explain that they are going to make a pretend pond
- Start by filling the tray with water, and slowly add the food colouring. Talk about what has happened to the water now
- Now, ask the children to add the stones and pebbles
- Go around the garden and find other things to add, such as twigs and sticks
- Lastly, put in the pond animals
- Ask the children to use their rods to see what they can catch!
- Leave the children to use their imagination and play with the pond
- Develop this by making a larger pond in the garden, using the paddling pool
- Take the painting easel outside – paint pictures of the pond and pond life. Talk about the animal, fish and insects that live in the pond.

Make a pond

More to explore

What you need:

- A small fish tank

- 2 goldfish

- Fish food

- Internet access

- Coloured pencils

What to do:

- Bring the fish tank into the classroom
- In small groups, look at the fish swimming around
- Talk about the fish – how they swim, the colours, etc
- Choose a name for the fish!
- Talk about what the fish need to stay healthy
- Show the children how to feed the fish – look at their food and how much they need
- Create a class timetable – giving every child the responsibility for feeding the fish
- Find some websites that have fish. Look at the colours and shapes of the fish
- Draw some different shaped fish and choose colours for them.

Home links

- Go for a walk to the local pond or lake. Feed the ducks together
- Visit the aquarium – look at different fish
- Research ponds and pond life on the internet

everything
early years

Make a pond

Enrichment Activities

The life cycle of the frog

What you need:

- A large fish tank

- Frogspawn

- Pond plants

- Magnifying glasses

What to do:

- Sit together outside on the grass. Introduce the activity by using reference books to look at the life cycle of the frog. Talk about the different key changes. Find out what frogspawn actually is

- Now take the tank outside. Carefully put some frogspawn in the clear fish tank, adding pond water and pond plants.

- In small groups, use magnifying glasses to explore the frogspawn. What does it look like? What colour is it?

- Record the changes that happen as the eggs hatch, introducing the children to key words:
  - Frogspawn
  - Eggs
  - Hatch
  - Tadpoles
  - Frogs

- Record how the tadpoles change – growing limbs.

- When the tadpoles start to get bigger, enjoy a trip to the local pond and release them. Discuss why you had to do that. What would happen if the tadpoles turned into frogs in the classroom?!

- Now, as a whole group, make a large wall display showing the life cycle of the frog: frogspawn – tadpole – tadpole with changing limbs – frog.

- Develop this - read 'The princess and the frog' together. Sing '5 little speckled frogs'. Talk about the importance of being kind and caring.

- Go on to investigate other life cycles, such as the butterfly.

Observations

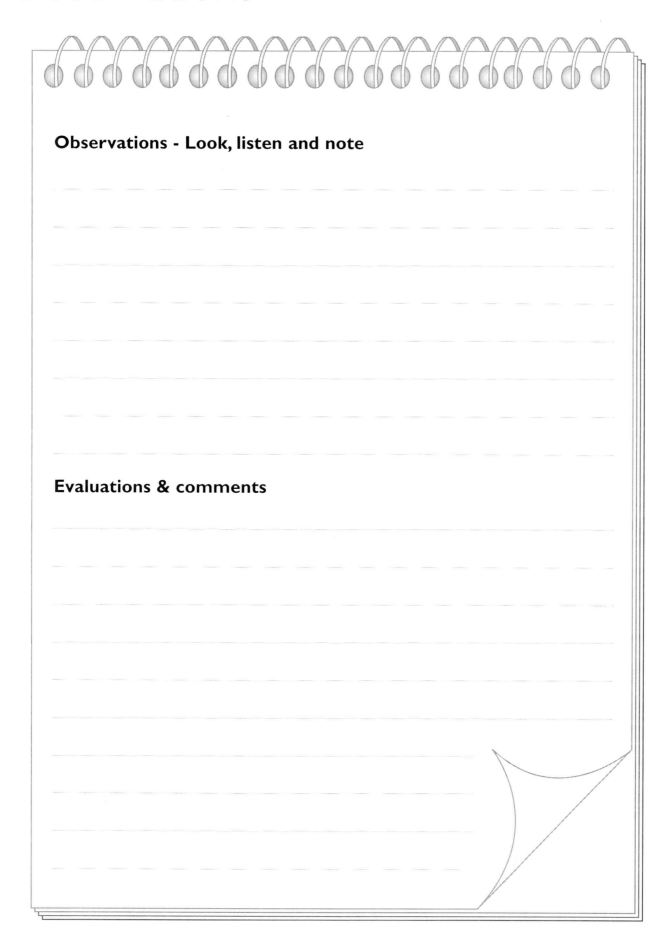

Observations - Look, listen and note

Evaluations & comments

The bird bath

What the children will learn:

- The children will enjoy working collaboratively

- They will recognise the importance of caring for other living things

- They will use an increasing vocabulary

Early Learning Goals:

PSED – work as part of a group, taking turns and sharing fairly

KUW – find out about and identify some features of living things and objects they observe

Useful Vocabulary:

- Bath
- Birds
- Feed
- Caring
- Wash
- Prey

Key activity – making a bird bath

What you need:

- A dustbin lid

- Pebbles and stones

- Bird seed

- Twigs

What to do:

- Take the children outside with the resources
- Explain to them that they are going to make a bird bath in the garden
- Turn the dustbin lid upside down
- Now, ask the children to use some large stones to help stabilise the lid
- Pour some water into the lid
- Ask the children to use the twigs, pebbles and other things from around the garden, to add to the bird bath. Make it attractive and safe for a bird
- Some of the children may like to use the twigs and leaves to make little nests around the bird bath
- Put the nests in quiet places, away from prey
- Sprinkle some bird food around the bath
- Sit back, quietly over the next few days. Do any birds visit the bath?

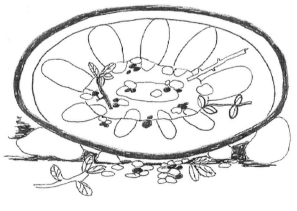

The bird bath

More to explore

What you need:

- Kitchen roll tubes and toilet roll middles
- Sellotape
- Acetate
- Scissors
- Elastic bands

What to do:

- Take the children outside with the equipment
- Explain that you would like the children to make pretend binoculars to look for birds visiting the bird bath
- Put two tubes together and attach with sellotape
- Put two pieces of acetate on the end and fix using the elastic bands
- Now, play with the binoculars!
- Can they spot any birds?
- What else could you design?
- Design a bird table that will hold a tin lid of water to drink
- Design a beautiful fountain for the birds to land on, to drink in or design a beautiful garden pond for the birds to use.

Home links

- Go to the local pet shop together and buy some food for the garden animals
- Visit the local garden centre and look at the bird products or the aviary
- Make a little bird house for the garden
- Have a bath yourself!
- Read books together about birds. Explore the different colours and shapes

everything
early years

The bird bath

Enrichment Activities

Wings

What you need:

- Pipe cleaners

- Tissue paper

- Glue

- Scissors

- Bird reference books

What to do:

- Take the children outside to look for different birds!

- As a whole group, discuss the different birds they may know and have seen in their gardens. Use reference books and pictures to help. Look at their beautiful wings. Look at pictures of the birds flying – how graceful.

- Now, talk about other animals and insects that have wings – such as the bat, the butterfly, ladybird and the bee. How many others can they name?

- What animals can they name that have wings but cannot fly – think about the penguin, ostrich and emu.

- In pairs, use the internet to research some of these winged animals.

- Now, in small groups, explore the dragonfly. Look at its four wings – how unusual.

- Using the pipe cleaners, ask the children to make models of the dragonflies. Encourage the children to bend and manipulate the pipe cleaners, making sure there are four wings.

- Now stretch the coloured tissue paper over the wings, and glue carefully into place.

- Hang the beautiful dragonflies around the classroom, from the ceiling

- Develop this - make a class poem together about the beautiful dragonfly, flying over the river

- Do an acrostic of a dragonfly, eg:

D azzling
R apid
A ngelic
G raceful ...
O
N
F
L
Y

using one word descriptions. Try some others.

Observations

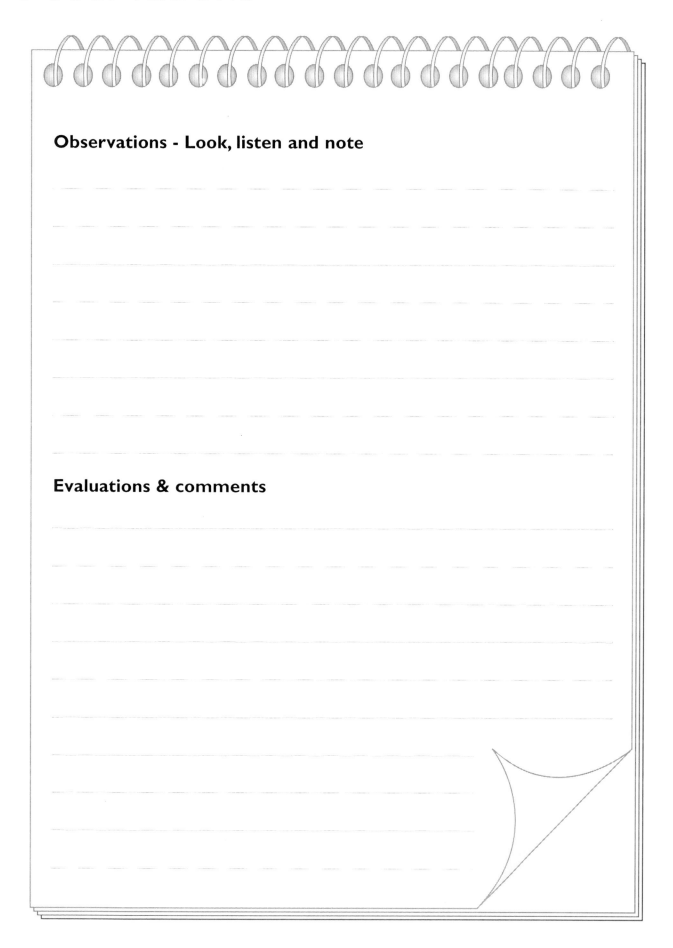

Observations - Look, listen and note

Evaluations & comments

everything
early years

Moving water

What the children will learn:

- The children will investigate water moving

- They will build and construct

- They will have the opportunity to work collaboratively, sharing ideas and taking turns

Early Learning Goals:

PSED – be confident to try new activities, initiate ideas and speak in a familiar group

KUW – ask questions about why things happen and how things work

Useful Vocabulary:

- Water
- Pour
- Up
- Down
- Top
- Bottom
- Slope
- Slide

Key activity – there's a hole in my bucket

What you need:

- Water

- Hosepipe

- Buckets, jugs and funnels

- Guttering

- Rubber ducks

What to do:

- Take the children and the equipment outside
- Introduce the activity by singing 'there's a hole in my bucket' and 'Jack and Jill went up the hill'
- Now, show the children all the resources available
- Talk about the resources, their names and their uses
- Ask the children to use these to build slides and slopes for the water to run down. Work in pairs
- Can they think of different ways to catch the water at the end?
- Talk about the water flowing down. How can they ensure there is always water at the top?
- Put the ducks at the top and watch them go down. Whose duck reached the end first? Race again
- Look for things around the garden that may float
- Experiment with these, keeping a record of what floats and what sinks
- Look at different water wheels in the water tray. Look at the water moving

Moving water

More to explore

What you need:

- Buckets of different sizes

- One bucket with a hole in it

- The water tray

What to do:

- Take a small group of children outside
- Ask them to play with the buckets in the water tray
- Fill the buckets – which is the biggest? Which would hold the most/least amount of water?
- Now, introduce the bucket with the hole, sing 'Theres a hole in my bucket...'
- Ask the children to investigate how they can move the water from one tray to another without losing too much water, using the bucket!
- Talk about the need to work quietly and why
- Is it better to use the bucket with the hole to move water or the new one without?
- Where could you put the hole to do least damage?
- Allow the children to experiment with the buckets to move the water.

Home links

- Enjoy finding out about floating and sinking during bath time
- Encourage the children to help wash the plastic dishes. Add washing-up liquid – look and play with the bubbles
- Work together to wash the car. Wash some garden toys

Moving water

Enrichment Activities

Discussion

What you need:

- Buckets

- Drainipes and guttering

- Watering cans

- Trays

- A bucket and rope to use as a pulley

What to do:

- Discuss water moving. How it flows downhill and needs to be 'caught' and 'carried' back up to its starting point

- Ask the children in pairs or groups to set up a large water run using drain pipes, guttering and chairs or stools to raise the guttering to different heights

- Watch the water move at different speeds. The children need to negotiate who will build the structure and who will pour the water.

- They can catch the water to re-use it. Perhaps they need a pulley, to pull the water back up to the top.

Observations

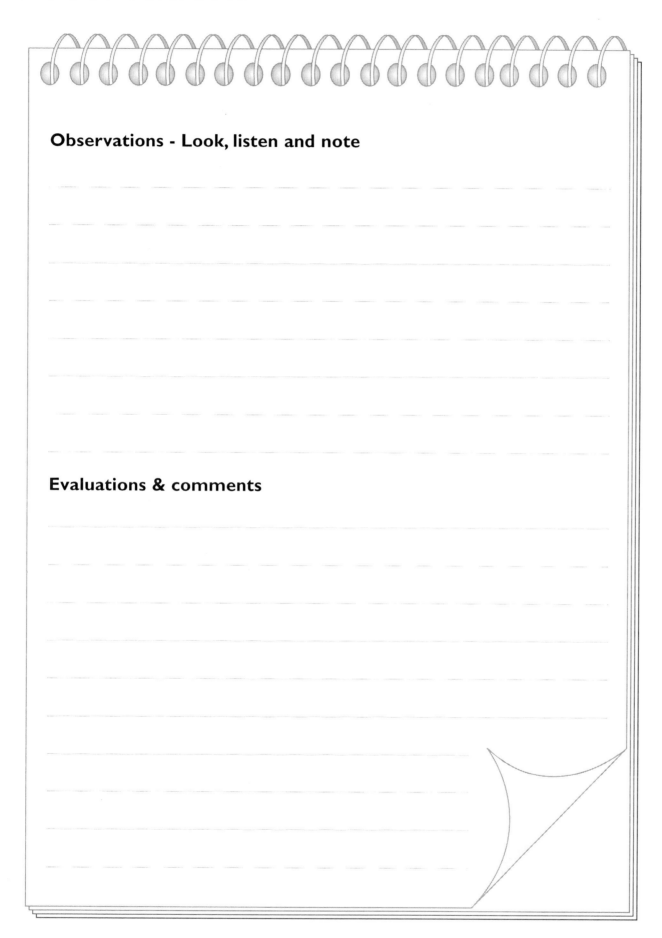

Observations - Look, listen and note

Evaluations & comments

Resources for outside play

Weather boxes

Sunny day storage box containing:

- Sun hats
- Sunglasses
- Beach towels
- Paddling pools
- Inflatables
- Fans
- Empty sun cream bottles
- Swimwear
- Buckets and spades
- Armbands and rings
- Water sprayers

Windy day storage box containing:

- Streamers
- Windmills
- Wind chimes
- Bubbles
- Kites

Cold snowy day storage box containing:

- Winter hats
- Scarves
- Blankets
- Sledge!
- Gloves
- Boots
- Buckets and spades

Rainy day storage box containing:

- Wellington boots
- Umbrellas
- Buckets
- Watering cans
- Brooms
- Large and small chalk and boards
- Rainy day books
- Rain hats
- Rain mackintoshes
- Jugs
- Cloths

Dark day storage box containing:

- Torches
- Coloured films
- Selection fabric
- Spare batteries
- Reflective materials
- Anything that glows in the dark

Cardboard boxes can be used for:

- Tunnels
- Buses
- Trains
- Building bricks
- Feely boxes
- Dens
- Cars
- Boats
- Post boxes

You can cut different size/shape holes and hide a variety of items and/or fill with shredded paper. Paint, chalk, crayon or stick on the boxes. Play hide and seek in big boxes.

Sand

Sand is a versatile resource. It can be used wet or dry, in large sand pits, troughs and trays.

For wet sand provide:

- Buckets
- Spades
- Spoons
- Rakes
- Flags
- Windmills
- Variety of containers
- Scoops
- Moulds
- Combs
- Shells

Children can experience filling and emptying, building castles, making patterns, digging, burying hands and feet, mark making in the sand. Treasure hunt / hide and seek games. Add cars, trucks, diggers or animals. Provide natural materials – stones, shells, twigs and leaves.

With dry sand provide:

- Sieves
- Strainers
- Jugs
- Containers
- Scoops
- Rakes
- Plastic or wooden animals
- Colanders
- Sand mills
- Buckets
- Spoons
- Spades
- Combs

Make sand shaker pots – like pepper pots. Bury hands and feet. Create a treasure hunt / hide and seek games. Add cars, trucks, diggers or animals. Provide natural materials – stones, shells, twigs and leaves. Add powder paint then mix and use for collages.

N.B. Be alert – sand gets in eyes easily!

Resources for outside play

Water play

Water play can be used in so many ways, but must be supervised at all times. A tap or water butt will allow for independent access to water. Provide any of these::

- Paddling pools
- Trays
- Bowls
- Watering cans
- Pots and pans
- Tea set
- Tubing
- Buckets
- Boats
- Bubbles
- Washing line
- Dolls clothes
- Large troughs
- Buckets
- Jugs
- Funnels
- Spoons
- Straws
- Plastic guttering
- A variety of brushes
- Fish and sea creatures
- Food colouring
- Pegs
- Sheets or blankets

Talk about floating and sinking objects. Add different coloured ice cubes and watch them melt!

Make a **bubble box** by placing a large plastic box on the floor with 10cm of water mixed with baby bath bubbles. Give the children plastic fly swats, place in the mixture and wave in the air.

Create themed water areas such as:

Car wash – ride on/in toys, buckets, bubbles, brushes, sponges, cloths and towels.

Laundry – buckets and bowls, bubbles, laundry, washing line and pegs.

Bathing babies – troughs/baths, bubbles, dolls, sponges, empty baby product bottles and towels.

Soil

Soil can be fun to explore. Provide a digging area, access to water and any of the following:

- Plant pots
- Jugs
- Spades
- Spoons
- Colanders
- Containers
- Trowels
- Scoops
- Sieves
- Bulbs, seeds and other things that grow
- Wheelbarrow
- Leaves
- Bark chippings
- Watering cans
- Magnifying glass
- Shells
- Animals
- Make mud pies
- Twigs
- Pebbles of varying sizes
- Cocoa shells
- Growbags
- Magnifying plastic box
- Construction vehicles
- Planting
- Dustpan and brushes

Create themed soil areas such as:

Garden centre – lots of different sized pots, soil, artificial plants and flowers, spades, wheelbarrow, watering cans etc.

A walk in the garden/grounds can be an exciting adventure. Explore the garden collect leaves, twigs, stones, flowers etc. in buckets and baskets- maybe use items in a collage.

Bug hunts – get down low, look up high, on grass, in corners and look for living things. Use jars with vents in to gather bugs then examine with magnifying glass or in a magnifying plastic bug box.

Tents, tunnels and dens

Gather together good materials for constructing dens and encourage children to bring things outside from indoors if they decide they need them.

- Sheets of material
- Boxes
- Rugs
- Sheets
- Staple gun
- Mats
- Pegs
- Blankets
- Sheer fabric or net curtains

Resources for outside play

Quiet areas

Quiet areas should be in the shade in the summer and sheltered on a winter's day.

Story fence/wall – laminate pictures or a book of children's work and attach to a wooden fence or inside play house or train. Use comfy cushions, mats or even a huge cardboard box and blankets on colder days. Use the area for books, puzzles, story-times etc.

Make a puppet theatre, provide puppets and story props in a box or bag.

Create a Velcro wall or board and encourage the children to find things that will 'stick'.

Sensory area

Sensory areas can be especially beneficial for babies and young children to stimulate their senses.

Laminate bright pictures and fix to fences. Put up wind chimes. Scented plants in cultivated areas and planters. Touch and feel boards and mats. Bottles containing natural materials, sand, stones, twigs, soil etc.

Music Area

A Music area can be louder outside.

Use everyday objects to make sounds. Hang instruments from a clothes horse. Provide a tape recorder and tapes, or a cd player and cds.

A list of inspirational music cds can be found in the Resources section on www.everythingearlyyears.co.uk.

Home corners and dressing up

Home corners and dressing up can be set up any where outside.

Create play houses and trains using benches, tables, chairs etc. Provide hats and dressing up clothes.

Utilise all your resources - use boxes, make a tent, have a camping theme or provide a steering wheel and number plate for a transport theme.

Messy play

Messy play is great to do outside – maximum pleasure, minimum cleaning!

There are many ways to set up and display messy activities when playing outdoors, not only at tables with chairs, but also try exploring on ground, walls, fences. Large play equipment and reflective surfaces add another dimension to the children's play.

Gloop

4 cups cornflour, 2 cups water and colouring. Use paddling pool, trays, troughs, jugs, containers, spoons, scoops etc. Explore with bare hands and maybe feet! Bingo, it just brushes off everything!

Jelly

Different flavours of set jelly in various moulds. Use in paddling pool, trays, troughs, with jugs, containers, spoons, scoops etc. Explore with bare hands and even taste. A great activity for the senses.

Pasta

Dry pasta can used in lots of ways – make shakers, collage, in trays, troughs, with containers, scoops, jugs etc.

Cooked pasta is a fantastic sensory experience, Use paddling pool, trays, troughs, jugs, containers, spoons, scoops etc. Explore with bare hands maybe feet or be really adventurous and let them sit in a paddling pool full.

Play dough
Uncooked dough
Mix 2 cups flour, 1 cup salt, 1 tablespoon oil, 1 cup water add colouring then knead until smooth.

Cooked dough
Mix in a pan 1 cup flour, 1 cup salt, 4 teaspoons cream of tartar, 2 tablespoons oil, 2 cups of water, colouring, then cook 3 – 5 minutes in a pan. Cool before use, can be stored in a bag in fridge.

Sand dough
Make a large amount using 5lbs of flour, sand, 5 cups of water, about 1 cup of white glue. Mix flour and sand in a large bucket or bowl, add the water until you have made stiff dough then knead with your hands until lumps have gone. Take a piece, then mould, shape, squeeze, pinch, prod, poke etc leave to dry, paint then varnish with diluted white glue.

Resources for outside play

Messy play continued...

Shaving foam

This is so versatile you can use it anywhere, and there is very little cleaning away to be done after. Squirt and have fun – have a foam party in the paddling pool or spray a trail for the children to follow.

Slime

1 cup Lux soap flakes, 2 litres warm water, egg beaters, whisks, scoops, ladles, jugs and aprons. Dissolve soap flakes in warm water and whisk until really frothy. Do not pour down drain after use – bag it and bin it.

Paint

Painting can be done on a grand scale outside. Using hands, feet and body, variety of brushes/rollers/sponges. Mix paint with washing up liquid to assist the rain or hose to wash it away afterwards.

- A roll of paper or old shower curtain attached to fence or placed over a climbing frame will allow for group painting.
- Cooked spaghetti dunked in paint and dropped on to paper.
- Paddling pool or large trough lined with paper – variety of balls and paint for giant marble rolling.
- Buckets of water and brushes to paint toys, fences, wall and pavements.
- Spray bottles with diluted paint and large papered area.
- Ride on toys through paint to make tracks on paper.
- Paint numbers or lowercase letters on the floor or wall.

Physical play

For physical play provide:

- Bats
- Quoits
- Skittles
- Large dice
- Floor mats and themed play mats
- Construction equipment
- Scoreboard
- Numbered bean bags
- Balls
- Hoops
- Bean bags
- Ropes and pulleys

Talk about running, jumping, hopping, crawling, slithering etc.

Books suitable for outdoor play

Messy Play
Noisy toys, messy toys – *Barbara Hunter*
Art – *Patrick McDonald*

Water
Whale – *David Lucas*
It's raining it's pouring, we're exploring – *Polly Peters*
Bog baby – *Glenn Millward*

Small World
Ten play hide and seek – *Penny Dale*

Music
Tanka tanka skunk – *Steve Webb*
Musicians of Brennan – *Child's Play*

Construction
Iggy Peck, Architect – *Andrea Beaty*
Michael Recycle – *Ellie Bethel*

Dens
Box – *Martha Lightfoot*
Not a box – *Antionette Portis*
This is our house – *Michael Rosen*

Movement and dance
Animal Boogie – *Debbie Harter*
Giraffes can't dance – *Giles Andreae*
Down by the cool of the pool – *Tony Mitton*

Listening
Polar Bear, Polar Bear what do you hear? – *Eric Carle*
Lullabyhullaballoo – *Mick Inkpen*
Noisy Farm – *Marni McGee*

Water
Daisy the doctor – *Felicity Brooks*
Master Track's train – *Allan Ahlberg*

Hands On!
Stuck in the mud – *Jane Clarke*
Mucky Duck – *Sally Grindley*

Wildlife
Arabella Miller's tiny caterpillar – *Clare Jarratt*
If only – *Neil Griffiths*
Ben plants a butterfly garden – *Kate Petty*

My own resources

My own resources

Summative assessments

Summative assessments

Plans for further activities

Plans for further activities

                                                                                   everything
                                                                                   early years